PAIN OF MY PURPOSE

How Faith and Fortitude Carried me through Chaos

TALSIA JENKINS

DEDICATION

I dedicate this book to God who is the head of my life, to my children: Kacie and Miley, Miller, and my sister, Nichelle Jenkins, to my nephew, Elijah, and to my nieces, Arianna, Amaya, Savanna Lowe.

To my extended family and friends who have prayed and believed God with me for the complete healing in my body. I want to say a big thank you for all your prayers, love, and support, it means the world to me. May all your lives be blessed forever. God truly has been faithful, and I am so thankful for all He has done and is doing in my life. I love you all from the bottom of my heart.

DEDICATION

TABLE OF CONTENTS

PRAYER

Father, I thank You for this beautiful soul that is reading this book, may their soul be blessed richly with my story. Lord, I give thanks for their lives and that You, God is glorified, not only will they be blessed by my story, but they will be uplifted and encouraged, and they will feel Your presence, that they too will experience Your healing hands, favor, love, and joy no matter what the situation is.

Father God, I humbly pray for all those that are battling with cancer, they may have just been diagnosed with this disease, Lord, for this beautiful soul to understand that the doctor's report is not final and that Your delivering power, is all they need to believe by Your stripes we are healed according to Isaiah 53:1, 4 and 5, I pray that You God will give them the hope and courage they need daily. Comfort them in their pain, and bless them with complete healing in the name of Jesus. Let them experience the joy You gave me, even when I wasn't feeling my best, give them the zeal to still get up and look pretty and face their Giants and leap over walls and slay their Goliath in the mighty name of Jesus. I pray for their family and loved ones, Father God, that You will lead them beside still waters and restore their souls and bodies. Lord help them to take this opportunity to draw strength and nourishment for the journey ahead. Lord, You are their healer and Great physician, help them to seek after You more so that they will cast all their worries and cares on You. Father, teach them what You wish for them to learn during these unpleasant times, help them not to take their discomfort out on those around them, and show them how to be a good patient while recovering, in Jesus' name I pray, Amen.

I AM AN OVERCOMER

T ell yourself that you are an Overcomer, it does not matter the battle you are facing, decree and declare it over your life right now at this very moment, and it shall be so in Jesus' name.

To my sisters who have survived Cancer: Woot! Woot! We did it, we slayed and beat our Giant, "Cancer." We are indeed OVERCOMERS! According to Revelation 2:7: You must understand this with every fiber in your body who you are. Let me be more in-depth in what I am revealing, an Overcomer is defined in the dictionary as "someone who prevails." And so, if we are going to rise above the hardships we face, we must fight to endure until the end and finish the course, we must overcome the challenges, we cannot give up, nor give in, fold, or bend.

For me to experience the manifestation of God's healing over my life; I immediately became a worshipper, I got closer to God, I learned to forgive, and this was important for me on my journey to healing. What we need to understand is, bitterness and unforgiveness can cause sickness, and it can eat us up spiritually like a cancer, and so I anchored myself into the Word of God, I did not forget who I was, and to whose I am, a Child of God and most importantly I didn't forget my responsibilities; yes, I rested, and yes I took out time for myself, but I was still a mother, a sister, an aunt, and a friend, I ensured I still enjoyed my life, I was very independent, I'm a giver, and naturally that's who I am, but the most important thing is that I did not withhold anything, and because of that I have seen God's unchanging hands, uncommon favor, unspeakable joy, and the peace He gave me in that season, oh my God, I cannot begin to express it-but if you understand this expression of "joy comes in the morning" feeling, then you will get the drift. So, these are some of the Characteristics of an Overcomer by trusting God with unwavering faith.

A LIFE A LONG TIME AGO

Our stories littering.
The meandering landscapes of our mind.
At times dark, at other's gold, glittering.
The past arrives in flashbacks.
Film reels of a life that's flown by;
like bullet trains speeding along their tracks.
Our former selves, a far cry
from whom we are now,
morphed from a caterpillar into a butterfly
O! Injured soldier, take a bow.
For the Lord created a galaxy,
and placed comet Chiron in its folds,
which soon became the wounded healer.
We read about, and hold
close to our hearts the lesson
that only folks who have been cut
deep with the knife of pain
knows what it is like to bleed,
and can give warm shelter to others in the rain.

I have often heard that we are creatures of our circumstances. Every intention, incident, and decision we encounter paves the way for our life's journey and brings us into the present.

Each person's life path is different, and our unique experiences culminate in the formation of our personalities, teaching us much about love, honor, integrity, and gratitude in the process.

People who have gone through immense pain often end up aging beyond their years. Sorrow has a nasty way of uprooting us. But we learn from it. The Japanese explain this concept beautifully through the art of Kintsugi–the mending of broken household items with liquid gold. For instance, you will find photos of ceramic pots with golden streaks running through them–a perfect metaphor for how the light only enters your soul when you have a scar that become entry points for the former.

When I look back at my life, I recognize that I have always navigated an uneven terrain, with jagged rocks jutting out from all corners of the roads I have been forced to travel. In hindsight, I realize that the only way I managed to weather the storms and shipwrecks of my life was by giving the steering wheel of my affairs into the Hand of God.

The trials and tribulations that impacted my life had started soon after my birth.

My mother had a complicated ectopic pregnancy. Struggling with crippling pain, she discovered that instead of growing in the main cavity of the uterus, I had made my way into her fallopian tube.

The aching would overwhelm her, to the point where three months into the pregnancy, her doctor told her that she could no longer carry me, and the best thing to do was to abort. With this devastating prospect plaguing her, my mother surrendered to God and asked Him for a miracle, as I was going to be her firstborn, and she didn't want to make the haunting decision of letting me go.

As fate would have it, the Lord gave my father the idea that a second opinion might help. And so, my parents decided to see someone who could join forces in faith with them and went to get spiritual advice. My father's recollection is murky at this point, but from what he does remember, my mother was instructed to drink six cups of hot water and a bottle of olive oil to find relief from the pain.

My mother, grasping at whichever straw she could find at this point, returned home, and told her aunt about the olive oil and water remedy. Encouraged by my aunt to try it out, my mother was fascinated when the process worked, and she found the pain receding within five minutes of ingesting the mixture. Her original doctor was amazed at the healing she experienced in such a short period and revoked the suggestion that the baby should be aborted.

In an absolute miracle, God held my mother's hand through the remainder of her pregnancy, and I was born on September 16,

1983, at Cornwall Regional Hospital in Mount Salem, Montego Bay Jamaica, as a full-term, tiny, but beautiful baby.

As the years passed and I moved through the milestones of girlhood, I realized that despite tragedy always skirting around my home, God was always on my side, making sure I was crediting myself for the strength I would forget I had.

Adversities lasted a lifetime. But when I think about the difficult times now, I know that even in the darkness, I was searching for the light at the end of the tunnel and embarking on a journey that would change my life for the better.

Three years after I was born, God blessed my mother with one more child-my little sister. Identifying with my sister as my partner in crime, I soon became inseparable from her, and I am glad I did, because a tragedy was about to strike, and we would need to be each other's armor to shield ourselves from the accompanying sorrow.

The first blow we dealt with came to us from our parents' separation. Going their separate ways, our parents left us without the family dynamics that my friends had the privilege of experiencing. But we sought refuge in knowing that our parents loved us dearly and had our best interest at heart.

In the aftermath of the separation, my mother started traveling extensively. Hence, she was never around to watch us grow up. However, I can't complain, because she made sure that we had a decent life, never lacked anything, and that we were well taken care of with a roof over our heads.

Therefore, we lived a normal life, but it was just never the same without our mother being home.

Sorrow came visiting like an old friend once again during one of her many travels. This time around, my mother decided to book a one-way ticket. As I waited for her to come back and tell me stories from whatever new land she had explored, I discovered that pining away would be of no use because she would not be coming back.

My mother migrated to the United States for good in the 90s. In her words, she wanted a better life for us, which explains the constant trips back and forth across borders. But one day, she disappeared from our lives.

I remember the sleepless nights that followed her departure. They would come and go, and often bringing with them agonizing crying spells, and the ghosts of memories I had from the time my mother had laughed with me, clung to my bedroom like a stubborn piece of wallpaper that refuses to be torn off.

To say that I felt rejected and unworthy in the years that followed my mother's absence would be an understatement. And as a young girl, I would often find myself struggling with a lack of self-confidence, questioning whether it was my fault that a parent figure exited my life. Loneliness was also difficult to meander through. With emotional debris everywhere, I felt like I had to clean up the mess all by myself.

It wasn't too long before my dad came to check on us. We were living with my mother's friend at the time, my father told us that he missed us and thought it was time for us to move on and that he is going to move back into the home we had all cherished together.

As a child, I had often hoped that just like my father reentered my life, my mother would too, and we would live happily ever after, in our Jamaican paradise. Eventually, I realized that my dad had to move on with his life. Soon, he got married to a beautiful woman. She was a businesswoman, and she made my father happy.

As I got older, I had to accept that I have a stepmother now, so as a child, I didn't quite know how to adjust to this new life. There were plenty of mixed feelings and uncertainty that made adjustment difficult for everyone. My father and my new stepmother did the best they could to raise me and my sister in the right way. I know my dad wanted the best for us growing up, he was very protective of us.

I can honestly say from the bottom of my heart that my dad did his best to always be there for us and gave us everything we needed to sustain ourselves. But it was just not the same without my mom. She was all I could think about. I wanted to be with her, and I craved her love and attention, her support, her encouragement, and her presence in our home.

Nothing compares to a mother's love for her family, and I knew my mother loved me and my sister. I remember when she would call us and as soon as the call ended, we would cry and long for her. It was an emotional time in our young lives, and we truly yearned to be with her every day.

I always admired my stepmother growing up, I cannot ever recall being disrespectful to my stepmother, but as a young child, I always thought some things were not fair. There were just some things we wanted to do as children but could not and so to make sure she was comfortable, I did my best to abide by the rules or suffer the consequences, and so if I was out of line, then we would indeed get punished which means I cannot ask to go anywhere or do anything with friends and that's how stern our father was with us. We were limited to watching TV or playing video games, we were not allowed to listen to secular music blaring on the radio as my father wanted to instill in us the importance of reading a book so that we can maintain good grades in school.

Many things were not fair, my father always advised me that before I left the house I should tell my stepmother, but when I did and when I got home, I would still get into trouble, and so it caused me to get to a very unhappy place in my life. It all just became too much for me, and I reached a point where I decided I didn't want to live at home anymore. I yearned to escape the feeling of being a caged bird and began to seek love and attention in the wrong places. Feeling lost and hopeless at a young age was very traumatizing, especially when you want what you want and not having anyone to really talk to, I became lonely, I felt unloved, I believe I experienced more sadness than happiness as a child and not understanding my emotions and able to cope with the expectations of me that were high.

HAILSTORMS ON THE HORIZON

I once heard that the late astronomer Carl Sagan describe the earth as a pale blue dot; a small insignificant speck lost in the folds of the enveloping darkness of our universe.

Poignant and profound, the idea that people create kingdoms off others' miseries, just to rule over tiny fractions of our tiny planet, stuns me, but life is what it is, and like everyone else, I too have lived through my share of thundering, uprooting hailstorms.

INNOCENCE LOST

Lauren Eden said, "When you're not fed love on a silver spoon, you learn to lick it off knives."

An ordinary quote, perhaps to some, but it shook the ground beneath my feet when I first came across it because it highlights my circumstances and resonates with me on a molecular level.

I mentioned before that while being broken, lost, and yearning for validation, I started to look for love in the wrong places. The account that follows meanders through the terrain where that decision took me.

Though young, I thought I was mature enough to know what I was doing. But I was wrong. Mixing with a dangerous crowd, I soon found myself at the wrong place and at the wrong time. At this point, I no longer wanted to be caged in like a bird, I wanted to be free, and so I would still find a way to escape and be free and do what I wanted. So, one night I decided to go hang out with my cousin's at a friend's house, there were a lot of younger guys at the house, and as I stood outside, there was an older man there who has now become burnt in my memory in the years that have passed. While other events fade from my mind, I can picture clearly that day. While I was hanging out; suddenly, I felt a tug as this man pulled me aside and told me he wanted to talk to me. In my young mind, I wasn't thinking, because now I just wanted to fit in. The sequence of events that transpired from this point on is blurry. As I fought to regain control over myself, this man took me into a room, and the next thing I knew was that I was being forced to lie down. I remember screaming until my throat began to ache, but no one was around. No one could hear my cries for help, and while I begged him to stop, he became even more aggressive.

The pain still lingers, from the day I felt my virginity slip away, taking my innocence along with it. With the bleeding and excruciating pain that came with the experience, I was no longer a naïve little girl, and as I struggled to cope with self-loathing, guilt, and confronting the universe for why it chose me for this annihilation of self-esteem, I realized I had just gone through an explosive coming of age. No number of showers could remove the traces of the act from my skin, and no bucket of tears brought me closure for a long time.

I couldn't tell anyone. As a victim, I felt scared of being blamed for what I had gone through, and so I hid the ordeal for a very long time. Eventually, I told my dad, and his response cuts me to this day. Recognizing that this was the reason I had stayed quiet for so long, I wondered why my father was so devoid of empathy and compassion for his child.

Dad was a stern, tough man, and all he wanted was to protect us, I know. But he showed his love in a different way – one that consisted of taking us to fairs and outings, and making sure that our material needs were fulfilled. But I could never talk to him. It was a hard pill to swallow when I was just 14, but it was a reality I had to learn to live with. After everything that happened that night, I became used to sitting outside on the steps of my house, and I remember speaking to God and asked Him to take me where my mom was, speaking it into existence.

BRONX BLUES

The year 1998 blessed me with my visa. Excited to leave my miseries behind, I felt like my greatest dreams had manifested into reality, and I could finally see my mother again. All set to go, I found myself on a plane in no time.

The plane landed at LaGuardia Airport, in Queens New York, on a cold winter day. My mom had come to pick me up, and my spirit knew no bounds to the joy I felt.

At the time, my mom lived in the Bronx with her husband, who had two children. Introduced to their pretty brick house, I noticed how quiet and peaceful it was, unlike the stern environment I was used to. However, I was with my mom, and that was all that mattered to me.

My mother knew this, and so she decided to keep me with her in the United States, and so I ended up staying in the country undocumented for a long time, which became difficult. When you do not have papers verifying your existence, you hardly have an identity, and it took me some time to adjust to my new life. Adapting to a new culture was not an easy transition. However, I had a stepbrother and a stepsister, so I had company, and we all had a good relationship, but my stepdad never really bonded with me. He was never around; he went to work and came home and showered and went back out, and so our relationship was really blurring.

Enrolling in high school took a whole year, it allowed me time to get adjusted into my new home and environment, and though I believe I had the patience and persistence to allow the process to work in my favor; I had to gain residency to become applicable for school, so until then, I was stuck in the house. When I gained residency, I finally enrolled in a high school called Evander Child, which is known for being one of the worst schools in the Bronx.

More of a prison camp than school, this place soon began to give me the creeps. Remembering how every day we had to go through metal detectors and get our bags searched and patted down is still painful for me as the scrutiny was not so prevalent in the culture I had originated from. But I learned to soften the blows through grit and resilience. I learned new skills as well while learning to navigate this foreign land on my own. For instance, taking the train was never something I had done before, but to survive, I had to embark on this adventure too.

The Bronx was a diverse neighborhood. Featuring people from all walks of life, it brought some comfort through the Jamaican food and things that I would eat back home. It was a very busy place, people always out and about–a city that never slept. Manhattan was close by, and what I loved most, was traveling there to shop and give myself some respite from the daily grind.

After school, I would walk home on White Plain Road, where most kids would get into fights. Time and again, I would see how people got jumped as part of a gang initiation. It was so crazy to me because I had never seen anything like it.

Wearing a clean slate as my badge of honor, I always prided myself for never being one to get into fights. But my classmates were followers of the violent crowd and wouldn't accept me for who I was. And thus, I became a loner, during my teen years, when all kids need the most support. Soon enough, my loneliness began to take a huge toll on me.

The culture shock was too immense. It forced me into a rebellion where I no longer wanted to stay in the United States. Missing my sister and my dad, I wished I could just go back home, and the danger of living in the Bronx just amplified this desire.

One life-threatening episode that fueled my apprehension for the Bronx stands out, it was a hot summer night; my stepsister, brother, and I, were sitting outside when a car slowly drove down the hill. It was dark, and the vehicle's windows were tinted. At first, we couldn't see anyone inside the car, the window tints were very dark, our internal alarm systems set our fight or flight mechanism into motion. But as the car got closer, all we suddenly heard were shots fired at us.

It was the scariest, most traumatizing thing I had ever experienced! In less than a few seconds, we were all on the ground, faces down. Thank God no one was hurt, but after everything we saw, especially the bullets that ricocheted off the grill fence, it shook us up that night. We never felt safe staying outside on the patio again.

And so, life went on, tainted by the blues that lingered around the blocks of the Bronx. It was not an easy existence at all. You had to be tough, street smart, and strong enough to brave the cold of its icy winters.

I had come to New York from a sunnier land, and the frost depressed me. Never could I have imagined that the wind could seep into my bones and make my teeth chatter so loud.

With all the adversity surrounding me, I ended up becoming a troublemaking, difficult adolescent, and staying out late became the norm, and I would often find myself outside the house into the darkest hours of the night.

My mother's attention too was diverted away from me. I started to notice that since my stepdad was never around, my mom was always occupied wondering what he was up to. This worked in my favor because I felt like I could just do whatever I wanted.

In the summertime, I would get invited to cookouts and parties, hanging out with my friends, I was having the time of my life, but eventually, my mom wasn't having it anymore, especially when one night I didn't come home and didn't even call to inform her as I only had a beeper and used payphones.

By now, my relationship with my mother had soured so much that I went to go live with my cousins in New Jersey.

My cousins had just bought a house in South Jersey, and I enjoyed my time there because I had my baby cousin whom I would babysit while his parents went to work. It was a welcome change to be around their family, we had great times, we went everywhere, being around extended family and getting to experience other places was a joy and so I thought perhaps it would be a great idea to relocate and live with them, amazingly they all agreed to the idea, and so I set out on my way to get my credentials from the high school I was attending, the process was not easy but I was able to transfer my credits and get back on track with school. With just one year of high school left to graduate, I was looking forward to things finally working out, unfortunately, things took a turn for the worse. The environment I was in, became hostile, and toxic, and my discomfort quickly led me back to my mother's house. I would never imagine things to be so, but it was better for me to be with my mother, it's not everything that glitters that is gold. I realized living in this country, people will tolerate you for a short time after which they change and no longer make you feel welcome.

IN THE MIDST OF THIEVES

When I went back home and my old ways manifested, fooling around with friends soon became a habit, as did staying out late.

My acting out upset mom to the point where one day, my stepdad and I got in a big fight. But, at this point, I had become a hardened, callous, young adult. I never listened to anyone's advice, until one day, my escapades led to getting robbed at gunpoint.

I had to beg for my life, and I knew it was a setup after it all transpired, I would never imagine this one, the innocence in my head of just hanging out with a friend who I thought was a friend and his cousin who had seen I had some jewelry, the greed for which made him hold a gun to my head. Choosing my life over some trinkets, I handed the whole stash to him and got a massive wake-up call.

I knew I had to leave New York now. I did not want to go to school anymore and was shaken up by the events that had taken place. Soon enough, I dropped out of high school, stayed in the house, and locked myself inside my room.

No matter what my mother did to get me out, it did not work. This was how I trudged on till I finally hit the age of 18 when I finally said it's time for me to go on my own, and so I went to live with my grandmother, leaving the Bronx behind, and never for a second, did I ever look back.

SUNSHINE FOLLOWED THE SHIPWRECKS OF LIFE

M y grandmother quickly became my rock–the anchor that kept me grounded as my broken spirit threatened to wander off once again, into the depths of despair.

I had a great relationship with my grandmother. Many late nights saw us talking away, discussing anything, and everything under the sun. I found a home in her, a shoulder I could lean on, a cathartic, restful resolution to everything I had endured all these years. Even today, I am grateful for the wisdom my grandmother passed over to me.

We spent most of our days together–my grandmother and me. She had the warmest smile and most comforting spirit. For an adolescent, staying on trend with the world is the one thing that matters most. And I know my grandmother loved me because she helped me become part of the hip, new American crowd, by buying me my first cellphone! Away with the beeper, this girl had the coolest grandmother a girl could ever ask for.

During this phase of my life, New Jersey greeted me like a wonderful new friend, and it didn't take me long to fall in love with the place. This colorful new city quickly became home, and I started reveling in the pleasure of being close to Manhattan where I could always run off to, to buy pretty new things on offer in the glass windows of star-studded stores. I did not have any friends, but these leisure trips into the Big Apple gave me respite and I made it work for myself.

More joy and healing followed. About two years after moving to New Jersey, my sister was able to come and join us from Jamaica, and I felt like my wounds were finally fully healing. My sister would be my best friend, and I could thrive in her company. I was elated.

It was even better than before, my sister and I now had more in common, for she had graduated from high school in Jamaica, and in the process, blossomed into a smart, competent young woman, with a good head on her shoulders. Having grown up, she would understand how life worked, and I could share anything with her. I was proud of her, for she had gone to a brilliant school—the result of my mother's heavy emphasis on quality education—and celebrated her achievement with great zeal.

Making her way to Jersey, my sister came brimming with memories from long ago, and I revisited them with her, as we chatted away about old times, filling each other in about all the adventures and miseries we had experienced since our separation. We realized that in navigating the meandering, confusing, painful, yet lesson-generating terrain of our lives; we had both come of age.

It was not long after (in fact, it was just a year!), that my mother moved to New Jersey with us. In a heartbreaking turn of events, she had found her husband was cheating on her and filed for a divorce. She was very big on loyalty, so when she found out, it hurt her to the core. I was so happy for her though because I applauded her for claiming her space, taking control of her life, and moving on from a marriage where she was not being treated right.

Those years in Jersey were some of my best. Living through them gave me renewed confidence in the healing power of the universe, and my self-esteem skyrocketed. I knew then, that despite the hardships that had tormented me for so long, I would get by in life, and make something of myself.

In mending my heart, I realized that I wanted to put the past behind me and move forward. My spirit became my guide–the North Star through which I journeyed to new opportunities.

Yet even though I was surrounded by hope and happiness, I felt like something was still missing. Perhaps it was the unfinished high school diploma, or maybe the desire for a chance to travel. I could not quite put my finger on it, but today, as I reflect on those years, I understand that my soul was yearning for a spiritual awakening–a deeper, more enriching connection with my Creator.

AT THE END OF THE TUNNEL, I FOUND GOD

My mother knew I felt empty, despite the peace that had followed the tumultuous times. She saw how much I would sleep to suppress the way I felt. My demeanor had started resembling something dangerously close to depression. One day, my mother decided as a family, we would be going to church. I agreed.

The church we visited is still etched in my mind today and constitutes a fond memory. I remember sitting in the pews when I was called to the altar and asked if I was ready to give my life to God. I was not. Not at the time.

Committing to living how God wanted me to, seemed too taxing back then, and I can recall being consumed by an all-encompassing fear that giving control of my affairs to my Creator would force me to give up all the worldly things I held dear.

My mind reeled with worry, and I anticipated I would have to change the way I looked, dressed, and conducted myself in social settings. In short, I was not ready to let go of living in sin.

However, church leaders are aware of the youth's affinity for sinful living, and hence they did not give up on me. Members of this church we had visited that fateful day set up a time to come visit our home for a Bible study session.

As the Church leaders sat with us, it was so refreshing to hear the Word of God. It made me feel like I did not have to have all the answers or all the solutions to my problems and gave me the confidence to note that a higher power was watching over me.

Being surrounded by people who were praying and uplifting us, and the words they used to do so, sowed the seed that fueled my passion for change in my life. My outlook on life shifted completely, and I began to look forward to walking with God.

The Divine works in wondrous ways, and He took my lack of belief and transformed it into a commitment to following His path. Soon enough, the day on which I decided to let go of the materialistic, superficial world came. I got baptized in the year 2004 and finally saw what I had been missing all along when I became a Child of God.

Like magic, things started to work in my favor. Just a few months after being baptized, I was able to get my work permit and social security number. Finally, I had the chance to work in America and secure my driver's license. My green card was still pending, but I was ready to get a job and strive for independence, something I had wanted since the moment I had set foot in this country.

My first job came through and it was a Sales Associate position at Sears in the Livingston Mall. We had gone on a shopping trip, all piled up on a bus, and by chance, I applied when I saw the store while walking around. I was hired on the spot! Isn't God amazing? It is less than a year after I entered the realm of belief, our lawyer who had been meticulously working on my case, called my mother, informing her that we had an interview appointment with the immigration office. My mother rushed to inform our church leaders, and we all stood in faith, praying for good news.

Preparing for the interview was daunting, but I managed to do it. My mother had to accompany me since she was the one who had filed the petition on my behalf. When we arrived for my interview, I was jittery with nerves, but I knew God would help me get through it.

I had expected the interview to be long and grueling. But to my surprise, the immigration officer asked me just one question, which focused on when I had last traveled. My answer was 1998– the year when I had first entered the country.

As soon as he heard my response, he stamped his approval on my papers, and just like that, I became a permanent U.S. Resident. It was, without a doubt, the best day of my life. I knew it was God's timing, and I could understand it now because giving my life to God had helped me see the truth about life with a pair of fresh new eyes, unwavering faith, hope for the future, and greater clarity.

FAREWELL TO THE NORTH - NEW DESTINATIONS

God makes miraculous plans. He knows how to align His children with people who will fill in the gaps when your faith is tested. Looking back now, I would not change anything, because everything that had wreaked havoc in my life, I had been delivered from them, and set free.

In 2006, I was able to travel back home after about seven years to see my father. By this time, I had put every difficult conversation behind and reconnected with him and my stepmother with a lot of love. I know now that even the tough moments I had spent with them as a kid were crucial in bringing me closer to God, so I was more than happy to stop dwelling on them.

My parents did not deserve my anger, I realized; the devil does, for it is he who rips families apart and forces people into conflict and chaos by unleashing his mischief into the world.

Renewing old friendships back in Jamaica was refreshing, and returning home made me realize I needed another change of environment.

We had created some wonderful memories in New Jersey as a family. But the environment of the city was no longer conducive for our success. We were really in a better place in God, but my mom decided that it was time to leave the North, head to the South, and start afresh. Once her divorce was finalized, she was ready to begin anew. So, in February 2008, we packed up all our clothes, gave away what we could, and relocated to Fort Lauderdale, Florida.

I was not too excited about the relocation initially, but I was open-minded. The hustle and bustle of Jersey and Manhattan had become like a second skin, and I knew I was in for a massive change.

However, as I lamented earlier, the cold in these cities would seep into my bones. I had always wanted to move to a better climate, and my chance to do so was finally here. Plus, I had always heard that if I lived in Florida, I would never miss the Island vibes that were reminiscent of my birth country.

With these thoughts swirling in my mind, I took the plane to this mysterious new State with my family. The plane landed in a city that was warmer and extremely welcoming.

Taking the cab to our new place, I was filled with excitement, and could not wait to explore this new region. Sunny Florida was very beautiful. In the early years, we stayed in a community that came complete with nice and quiet homely villas. I was not used to not seeing people, so it was very different for me.

After a few months, I got to witness the beauty of South Florida. The weather was perfect, so I did not waste any time and soaked it all in. At the time, I lived closed to one of the biggest malls in my neighborhood-Sawgrass Mills-and within two months of moving, I applied for the position of a Sales Associate at Nieman Marcus Last Call. This job helped me save enough money to buy my first car. My 1998 Chevy Cavalier was a lovely vehicle, and I was so proud of myself for having become capable enough to afford it. My mother was ecstatic too and hurriedly bought four new tires for my car. Things seemed to be going well. We still did not quite have it all together, but we loved each other, found joy in little things, celebrated every tiny victory, and made the best of each day.

THE FLOOD AND THE FALLEN

B elievers are often met with trials. It is God's way of polishing our souls and strengthening our resolve. My trials came beckoning once again, this time in the form of disease and death.

My mother had married again; this time, she had met a very nice, humble man, and we felt like she was finally getting to live stress-free. However, right after their wedding, her husband became very ill. He spent months in the hospital due to kidney failure, followed by dialysis, and it was a very testing time for us all.

Of course, my mother felt the impact more deeply than the rest of us, and she tried to spend as much time with her husband as she could, but the worst was yet to come. In the months that followed, my mother herself became very sick. We did not know what was wrong with her, but she would be in so much pain that I had to rush her to the hospital several times.

The doctors ran many tests and admitted my mother to the hospital. Eventually, we found out that she had gallstones and needed a cholecystectomy to remove her gallbladder. The surgery went well, and she was discharged from the hospital a week later. We all thought that the storm had passed, but when she came home, the illness took over again.

My mother's eyes began to display a yellow tinge, and she started complaining about severe stomach pain. That day, Broward General Hospital saw us rushing through the corridors looking for someone who could help my mother. The doctors ran a scan on my mother and discovered that complications from the surgery had caused injury to the bile duct, the intestine, bowel, and blood vessels. Together, these fatal injuries had caused a leak that poisoned her body.

Another surgery to be performed in the ER. As my mother laid recovering from it, I decided to go home and freshen up. I remember that she called me from her hospital bed, inquiring when I would be returning to see her. I had told her I was just about to be on my way. Never in my wildest dreams could I have imagined that this phone call would be the last time I would be hearing my mother's voice.

Within an hour of the call with my mother, I received another call from the hospital. I was not even fully dressed when a doctor's voice asked if I was sitting down. I answered in the affirmative, after which the doctor proceeded to tell me that my mom had passed away.

Perhaps it was on the day of my mother's death I truly realized how it feels when the floor shakes beneath your feet. The doctor who broke the news to me made a Herculean effort to comfort me, but of course, it did not work. I was told that during the recovery phase, my mother had gotten a heart attack. The medical team did everything it could to resuscitate my mother, but when God has called His people to Him, we are powerless against His decisions.

I remember the phone dropping from my hand and the stream of tears that sprung from my soul. I cried like a wounded animal, but God must have given me extra strength to bear this news because I was the first one to receive it. My sister had not been home at the time. She had gone to pick my stepdad up from his routine dialysis appointment, and so I did not want to call her while she was driving.

When my sister returned home with my stepfather, I told them both to sit down and then broke the news. It was surreal, I could not imagine something like this would ever happen, but it did. Helplessness is the only way I can describe the state we were in. As clear as day, I can recall holding onto my stepfather's legs and weeping, wondering if the pain would ever heal. Guilt also gripped me, and I beat myself up for not having stayed with her longer.

But it was time for the final goodbye. We got ourselves together and rushed to the hospital in a daze, barged into the room where they had her body, and just stood there reeling. I truly felt like a motherless child seeing her body just lying there. I remember feeling like there was a strong presence in the room, but when I touched her body, it was cold. I just wished at that point that she would wake up. I have never felt such pain in my life.

I know we all must depart this earth one day, and death is a reality we have to face. But with my mother's passing, it became a concrete thing for me.

My beautiful mommy, may her soul rest in peace, left her memory deeply carved into my soul. My late mother Sonia Lawrence passed away on December 10, 2009. She had a beautiful funeral; I saw many family and friends gathered from near and far. We celebrated her life and her beautiful spirit.

My mom was a Woman of God and I am so grateful to God I got to witness her journey and bask in her glow. All these years, she helped make life a little better for my sister and me, doing everything in her power, and with God's help, to make sure we never lack anything. She was sweet, humble, and very kindhearted, and I will always remember our powerful connection–the good times, the laughter, and the lessons. We had made the best of each day. It was never a dull moment when she was around.

My grandmother's only baby girl. It was indeed one of the hardest things to bury my mom. As the casket was lowered into the grave, reality kicked in. At that time, my sister and I wanted to go to the grave with her. It was so tough. No one wants to lose their loved ones. I could feel my heart exploding.

As I sit here remembering the old days, I can recall how my mother and I had been best friends. The world had largely left us to our own devices, and we had to lean on each other to get through. We used to do everything together. I would talk to my mom about everything. She was a funny, a loving woman who loved the Lord.

MY FAITH TESTED

My mother's passing made me nonchalant. As I grew numb with each passing day, the hardships of life started peaking from the corners again, tempting me to return to my sinful ways. It was not easy. I felt like a lonely child who was lost, a long way from home. Soon enough, I stopped going to church and started doing what I wanted to do. I did not care anymore about any consequences or the stunting of my spiritual growth. I disconnected myself from everyone. You would think that in my loss and moment of grief, I would draw closer to God, right? No, I dealt with my mourning the complete opposite way, my soul was lost, I was a wreck. On top of losing my mother, the church was not a safe haven at all, it's a sad thing to say, but it's the truth.

THE GIFT OF A CHILD

After my mother's death, I started to date. I met a guy; a single dad with four children, who was raising two girls on his own. When he told me how many children he had, I had brushed him off, because I was afraid to get involved with someone who had children.

He pursued me however and did not give up until I finally let him take me out on a date. For the first time, in a long time, I decided to let my guards down and let him in, realizing that it would not hurt to take a chance at love.

We dated until our relationship got serious, and I later found out that I was pregnant with our oldest daughter, Miley.

The news came as a life-changing recognition that I was about to be blessed with a little soul whom I could love and cherish. For me, this was the brightest ray of sunshine the universe had ever bestowed.

I had always wanted kids, but I never thought I could conceive. I was 28 at the time when I found out I was pregnant. It was a good pregnancy, without any complications up until my daughter's due date when my Ob-gyn (obstetrician-gynecologist) decided to induce labor because it was past the expected delivery time.

The midwives watched how far I was dilated, but sadly I had to have a Cesarean delivery (C-Section) the labor was not progressing, and there were fears that a stalled labor might cause the baby distress, which could result in changes in her heartbeat. So, a C-section was the best option.

On November 25, 2011, my beautiful baby girl was born. She was just perfect! With her thick, soft, black hair that lay flat on her head, she was the sweetest little child, and I remember being awestruck and engulfed by gratitude to the Creator.

I was a mother now. My womb was blessed. My daughter was such a little angel, and I was honored that God would choose me to be her mom.

When Miley was born, we were still living in the same house that my late mother, sister, and stepdad shared, but change they say is constant and so we all decided to move, and go our separate ways, and the next few months saw me moving in with my in-laws. My sister went to New York City, and my stepdad rented a room here in Florida.

ONCE AGAIN – TURBULENT SEAS

I was not too keen on living with my in-laws, but my youthful and humble bank balance left me with few choices. I had to make it work.

As my partner and I spent the next few months trying to save money for our place, it became increasingly uncomfortable to put up with our current living conditions. While I was grateful for a roof over my head, I started running into a very rough patch with the father of my child.

Looking back after all these years, I think that perhaps feeling alone and unsupported are two of the worst emotions you can encounter. If you can make peace with them, you have weathered a great big storm.

At this point in my story, I had learned to greet these emotions as old friends and knew them better than the back of my hand. This time, they manifested in long days where my partner would leave me all alone in the house to look after the baby.

As the days stretched into weeks, I remember feeling completely disconnected from the man I had loved and whose child I bore. I began to sense he was having an affair behind my back. His frequent outings rang alarm bells in my mind real loud.

One fated day, we got into a huge fight. In the aftermath, I must have thought that things were broken beyond repair because I packed all my belongings and scrambled to New York. I knew no one in Florida, so the city that had served as my former home would have to be the place I returned to.

In the Big Apple, a very good family friend welcomed my daughter and I to her house. I was utterly grateful. I knew I had rushed into things, just leaving my partner like that. However, I had been too unhappy for too long and needed to be closer to my sister, who would help me raise my little girl. My partner did not seem like much help back then.

I was ecstatic that my sister would be with her niece. Both loved each other just as much, and as my sister started lending a hand in Miley's upbringing, I also developed a deeper bond with her.

It was not an easy transition. I had to face the reality that I was a mother who had to do whatever she could to survive for her daughter and herself. The separation was tough, and on several occasions, I found myself thinking a child needs her father in her life. However, I could not spend too much time indulging in these thoughts because I had other issues to worry about.

It started with a severe body ache. Miley was about four months old at the time. I did not know what was wrong with me, except I was in too much pain. I felt very sick. No matter what I ate, it would come right back up. I would lay upside down, and the pain would get even worse.

Immediately, I called my sister and begged her to take me to the hospital.

Upon reaching there, the doctors ran scans, did some tests, and gave me an official diagnosis. I was struggling with the same illness that had afflicted my mother–gallstones. I was admitted on the very same day.

The doctors told me I needed surgery, and it was the same thing that my mother had gone through. So, I was in the hospital for a whole week before they operated on me.

I consider myself a strong woman. Even while lying on that hospital bed, I knew I was not going to let my condition defeat me. I had to fight, and I was ready for the battle. God became my armor, and the surgery ended up being successful.

Once healed, I was released and sent back home to my baby. After all the medication I had received, I was not able to breastfeed my child. By now, she was used to drinking formula. She was in my sister's capable hands, which have always remained a tower of strength and resilience.

However, soon enough, I started to realize I could not raise Miley alone. New York was not the same after 9/11. I was not used to how the city operated now and realize raising a child in this big city by myself would take a toll on me.

Following this realization, it did not take long for me to decide that her dad needed to be around. He missed her a lot; plus, I had never wanted my child to come from a broken home. Hence, I did everything I could to make amends, it didn't take long, and we moved back to Florida. Miley's dad was happy to have us back, and we decided to make each day worth fighting for. We stayed together for many years after this reconciliation. My partner went to great lengths to make sure we remained a family, and I never denied his love. He did not have a lot to give to us at the time, but he did his best to make ends meet, I never judged him or looked down on him.

Still young and learning, we did the best we could. I always believed in the power of prayer, so I knew I had to keep praying for forgiveness, for God to help us because we were not married. I always felt bad because we were living in sin, but I was not ready for marriage.

Living with my in-laws took a toll on my health. We needed more space and privacy. I would get so stressed that I started to have terrible headaches; they were so intense that I could not function like a normal person. I would be at work when these headaches would happen. It felt like my head would pound off my body.

I did not want to dwell on the pain but knew something was not right. I knew I had to schedule an appointment with my primary care doctor.

Once I visited the doctor, he told me that my blood pressure was very high. According to the doctor, I could die at a very young age if it's not treated. I was told to manage my condition by learning to de-stress, exercising, and eating right. I was also prescribed daily medication.

After learning about this new diagnosis, my partner and I decided to start going out more often. We would get out of the house by going to the beach. Every weekend, we would go to the mall. Self-care became extremely valuable to me.

A GLIMPSE OF RELIEF

We weren't married yet, and I knew he wanted to be married, and he showed how much he cared for me and truly wanted us to make our relationship work, but to be honest, I was afraid of getting married and end up getting hurt. For a long time, I ran away from marriage because I was already in a hard place, and we had so many things we needed to work on.

Thankfully, he was patient with me, and over the years, we continued to work on strengthening our relationship. We knew that we needed to be in our own home and raise our family. So, for a few years, we worked on strengthening our relationship. We also went around house hunting.

I decided to reach out to my sister and ask her how she felt about the possibility of sharing a two-story townhouse for one year. She thought it was a good idea because she and her husband were also looking for a place to live as well. I was so happy I was finally moving out of my in-laws.

Our relationship had gotten better. We had gotten closer, and our minds were blooming along with our health. By this time, we had also started going out on dates and reveling in each other's company.

My partner and I decided to get married. We set a date, and on September 20, 2014, I was walking down the aisle. We made our vows to each other on the beach, in the presence of close friends and family members. The ceremony was followed by a reception held at a hotel in his hometown.

Every young married couple goes through the woes of domestic life. We did too. Within a year of our wedding, we had to move back to my mother-in-law's house, the same one that we had left all those months ago.

The move was necessary because of the issues we started to experience, such as high-power bills and electrical issues in our apartment. Bug infestations were forcing us to throw our belongings away, and the general environment of the home was uneasy. A combination of all these factors finally called upon us to break the lease and move out.

Within six months of living with my in-laws, my husband found a brand new two-story townhouse that was just built with a garage in a gated community.

This new home greeted us like the perfect dream, and I believe God had honored our marriage by gifting it to us. This house gave us a chance to settle down. It was a sign we deserved good things in life. We had sacrificed a lot to come to this joyous place. So, we gathered the money required for the deposit and moved in.

CLOSETED SKELETONS

The first year in this beautiful house was wonderful. Its corridors gave Miley a maze to run through, and the bedrooms emanated a glory I was proud to rule over. However, after we celebrated our second anniversary, the old skeletons started to emerge from the closet.

My husband and I started to have irreconcilable differences, which ultimately manifested into infidelity and a lack of forgiveness, which culminated in a divorce.

I really wanted my marriage to work. We had been through so much together, and when we decided to get married, it was an ode to the idea that we would grow old together. However, some things were out of our control. The force of nature had gotten us this far, and now, it had bid us farewell. We had slowly but surely hit a brick wall.

I remember how mercilessly we used to fight. There even came the point where my husband told me to leave his house. How dare him to tell me to leave, after all that we have been through. Why wait until now to show this side? I did not need to be told twice. Nursing my wounded ego, I packed up and left.

At that time, I remember feeling completely hopeless about life. I had started to realize that what was happening was bigger than me. I had no strength to keep fighting and be rejected.

When I left that house, I felt wrecked. I was crying all day and night. I did try reaching out to my husband, but he had become very angry towards me, and I knew we could not fix things.

I had unconditional love, but I felt like he did not have the patience, love, and compassion towards me anymore for us to thrive. I know many relationships hit rock bottom, but this was the pit.

Over the years, all I wanted from my husband at the time was his support, understanding, and compassion. I wanted him to be empathetic towards me. I remember being tired and feeling sick every other hour. I would be drained after cooking, cleaning, and making sure the family was taken care of.

Still, my husband would get frustrated with me. Eventually, we both had lost touch with expressing what we felt without it turning into a big fuss. There was no balance in the home and communication was as if I was walking on eggshells when it came to certain situations. That marriage taught me a grand lesson, one that encouraged me to reclaim my life by surrendering it to God. Only the Divine could restore everything I had lost.

After all the horrible things I had encountered, I felt like I was losing my mind. The domestic warfare was strong, and my only hope was to surrender myself back to the Lord because the enemy was out to destroy me.

Amazingly, as I grew closer to God, He sent the right people to me in the nick of time. During this period, I was introduced to an ordained church which had a counseling and deliverance service. After meeting the pastor, his wife, and other members of the church, it felt like God was connecting me to the right people Himself. These people helped me get through the toughest period of my life, and I was able to get the spiritual enlightenment and deliverance I needed to prepare me for the next chapter of my life.

I remember every tear I shed while praying for deliverance as the little girl in me felt the hand of God healing my broken soul. I knew that the Lord will not leave me in vain.

Through the grace of God, it was not long before I started to see a change in my husband. When I left our home, my husband got close to one of his daughter's friend's mother, I did not want to believe it. I met this woman once. In actuality, we invited her so we could meet her since her daughter wanted to spend the night at our house and that was that, just to show you how the enemy likes to put his head into our affairs, and yes I left the house, but already she was becoming his emotional backup, a rebound is what I called it, but he is still married. What kind of woman I said to myself would want to have a relationship with a married man? Well, I knew one way or the other, he had to break things off and leave this woman alone. The warfare was real but I continued to pray and trust God, eventually, he broke things off with her, I remember him telling me that he got to see a side of her he did not like, realizing how selfish she is.

What had opened his eyes was one night when this woman came to our home drunk and threw up in our bathroom. He was not used to this kind of atrocious behavior, especially when she displayed it in front of the children.

I do not live my life so raucously, so seeing someone indulge in reckless behavior turned my husband off but after that ordeal, my husband and I had a lot to work on. There were many open wounds in our marriage, scars, and gashes that could become fatal if we do not treat them with care. We battled with a lot of demons lingering around to really destroy us. I can recall some of the most painful things I had experienced when he would give me a gift, like a phone or a piece of jewelry, and then he would take it back later. I was emotionally abused by him. Sometimes, I felt he had used his power to intimidate me because he knew I had nowhere else to go and no one to turn to. He always took advantage of that.

However, I never backed down or submitted to anyone belittling me and making me feel like they can treat me however they want; and because of this, I had to learn to take back my power from the enemy. I now realize that after going through those difficult times, it was not him I should have been upset with, but the devil. I understand now that the enemy does not like marriages, and because I was not praying effectively, the doors of infidelity remained open, and that devil had legal grounds to destroy our marriage.

I had gone through some tough times is an understatement at the very least, but I stayed and hoped for things to get better.

It brought some closure when my husband admitted he had an affair with his high school sweetheart and the mother of his oldest children. When I met my husband, they had not been together for many years, in fact she was in a relationship, and I could not even have imagined that their paths would cross once again, because in his words they both hated each other.

THE SHELL SHOCK OF A MARRIAGE ON THE ROCKS

Their paths did cross–the road my husband was on, and the alleyways his former flame walked intersected in my absence with such flair that discovering the truth about the unfaithful acts my husband had been indulging in behind my back shattered me.

To my dismay, I was informed that when I had left, the woman in question had started to come around more often to help take the children she had mothered to school. One thing led to another and her reconnection with my husband culminated in sex. When I confronted my husband about this, he responded by saying that he and I were separated anyway so I cannot hold him accountable as he was no longer answerable to me.

A woman's heart though is a loyal place, and in my head, my husband and I were still married. I knew I would never stoop so low as to cheat on him when in the eyes of both the law, as well as our religion, we constituted a partnership.

So, knowing he felt otherwise was perhaps the final nail in the coffin that housed my soul that continued to succumb to its emotional wounds. For many months, I found myself questioning why another woman would barge in and occupy my husband's attention, why it had to be the girl he loved back in adolescence, and why now when she had been with someone else for so long.

The fighting between my husband and I became increasingly unbearable, and once again my husband told me to leave the house and that I should leave the keys on the counter. I did exactly that, for I was too tired of the constant emotional abuse.

Plus, I realized that by this point, my husband was so smitten by this woman that he was too blind to see the only reason she was driving a wedge between us was that she wanted what we had.

After all, why didn't she profess her love a long time ago? All these years, she had not even bothered to keep in touch. Now, she was driving the car my husband had gotten for me, making regular visits to our home, and slowly but surely creeping back into my husband's heart.

I was aware of this woman's history of unfaithfulness in love though. I also knew that she had been in and out of relationships, been extremely promiscuous, and had never stayed loyal.

Knowing everything I knew, I realized that what was happening was an attack on my marriage, an occurrence that was most likely a test. I was expected by the Divine to pass.

God does cause it to rain on both the just and the unjust, but everything about this was wrong. On cold nights, as I sat sobbing, I poured my heart out to my husband and begged him to tell me how he knew this woman's intentions were not filled with malice.

I would highlight the fact he had never trusted her before and wondered how he was not suspicious of her anymore.

I would vocalize that this woman knew my husband's weakness was sex and she could easily seduce him to get what she wanted, especially monetary support since she had never thought twice about my husband in all this time yet now, she was back like nothing had broken between them in the past.

Of course, I understood all too well that this woman had children with my husband and had wanted to play her role as a mother, but the reality I was confronted with was painful to the core, particularly because my husband had always told me he would never reconsider a union with this woman when any topic related to her had come up while we were married!

Maybe I had been too blind to see the signs. Naturally, I was so shocked to the point of utter despair, but the tiny voices in my head told me I had always known my husband to have a special place in his heart for this woman, and that in his books she could get away with whatever she wanted.

This woman and I had never gotten along, especially now that we were married. No matter how nice I had been, she had never accepted I was in her children's lives.

Even though as a stepmother, I had done everything I could– showing my stepchildren love, and treating them like my own, I had never been viewed admiringly by their mother, whose disregard for me trickled down to the young ones too. They did not want me to talk to them most of the time, and starting a conversation was like walking on eggshells. It was tough, but I continued to do my best as the years passed.

Eventually, I recognized I'd had enough of my home being wrecked, and decided to take matters into my hands. I reached out to my husband's new girlfriend, and confronted her about what exactly it was that she wanted with my man. To nobody's surprise, she did not care she was being called out for destroying someone's marriage. In fact, she told me she enjoyed what she was doing to drive me away from my husband and told me things I had only confided in him about.

Knowing that along with my heart, my husband had also broken my trust was perhaps the biggest betrayal I had ever faced.

Yet, when this woman realized my husband had divulged her secrets to me as well, she began to fume and got into a big argument with me. I, on the other hand, was shocked she was still going to stay by my husband's side, even when he had not respected her privacy. Perhaps because she made it clear to me he was taking care of her and her daughter.

My husband and his former lover had been having sex whenever I used to be home with the kids. During these occasions, they would meet up, and she would start on her mission to rip my marriage apart. I remember she gave me many labels, she called me names as though she was better than me; names such as you stupid Jamaican, and I do not know how to keep a man, and she vouched that she and him will never break up, once he divorces me, the devil was truly at work in her, and that is why today I forgive her, the poor soul doesn't understand what she has brought on herself.

With my world falling apart, I gradually began to realize that karma works in strange ways and makes an appearance when you least expect it.

Now this woman had a lover that had no idea what was going on, only that she was supposed to be taking the children to school. It came to my knowledge the lover did not like what was happening, and gave this woman an ultimatum. If you recall, my husband had given out my car to this woman to take her daughters to school, and one day she took the car and left him, never to come back, until a few days later, she sent the car back, and went back to her lover. At this moment in time, my husband felt betrayed, as he realized that this woman had been playing games on many fronts.

DELIVERANCE

While separated from my husband, I took the time to work on myself and heal from the pain I was batting with. The feelings of unforgiveness, hurt, shame, regret, and uncertainty, had become deeply rooted in my soul, and I am grateful turning to God helped me to let go of them, as they did not belong to me. I was surrounded by the faithful, so it did not take as long as I anticipated to get back on my feet.

These compassionate friends prayed for me with vigor and helped me internalize the truth, that while I am far from perfect, I have a good heart and good intentions and I truly meant well.

It was tough of course; I knew I had to get delivered from the Generational curse. I had to break free and learn how to forgive those who had wronged me. At the time, I was also battling with rejection, but I kept fighting my way through, after much needed help and prayer, I became free and sanctified.

A MIRACLE CHILD

While caught in the throes of my tumultuous life, I started to realize how emotional I would get. One fateful day, I was watching TV and started crying for no reason at all. This was around Christmas time in 2015.

As the tears began to flow, I just knew something was different, I had missed my monthly menstrual and decided to take a pregnancy test. To my complete surprise, the test turned out to be positive and I was over the moon.

When I shared the news of a new child with my husband, he was not happy. In a fit of anger, he demanded I get an abortion, that broke my heart to pieces. For me, this was out of the question. I had promised the Lord I would never do something like that. So, if my husband did not want to be with me, that was fine, but the baby was staying.

With firm resolve, I made up my mind that come what may, I would be having another child, even if it meant I would have to navigate my second pregnancy alone. By this time, my faith in God had strengthened so much I knew He would support me through the challenge, even if my husband was not in the picture.

The notion of fathering a child, however, often makes men see the error of their ways as they start to recognize their home is about to be inhabited by a new impressionable infant. Perhaps it was this realization or just pure magic, but following the news I was pregnant, my husband broke any remaining threads off with the other woman.

I remember it clear as day, the way my husband told me he would never see this woman again, because he knew now he had been in the wrong. Confiding in me, he had cried and held me as he kissed my stomach to apologize. This was all well and good, but I started to consider giving him one more chance when he requested, we keep trying to mend our relationship by visiting a counselor.

For a long time, I had known my marriage was standing on shaky foundations, so I agreed, and we found a faith-based counselor to guide us through the hardships we were facing. Delighted that we were finally going to get some much-needed help, we setup a good date and time for our first session and proceeded to talk to the professional about the issues we had.

Not all professionals are experts at their jobs though, and this became evident quick with regards to the counselor we were visiting. With a heavy heart, I recall what this person had said to me when I told him my concerns. Point blank, like it was no big deal, verbatim he had said to me: "So what if your husband had sex with another woman, you need to get over it."

Devastated that a counselor could operate without even a shred of empathy, I had stormed out of his office with my mind reeling with humiliation, sadness, and just plain confusion.

In the aftermath of the utter failure that counseling turned out to be, I decided to focus my attention on looking after myself, to ensure the healthy birth of my second child.

Sorrow has a way of finding you, though if testing the waters have not been navigated thoroughly and carefully. In my story, I realized the threads my husband said he had severed with the other woman had perhaps not been cut off properly. She was back in our lives as swiftly as the rain pours from the sky.

One day my husband came home late, and immediately, I knew something was off. Call it a woman's intuition, but I could smell disloyalty on his clothes. Trying to keep the peace, I casually asked him where he was coming from, and he responded by telling me he had been visiting his mother's house.

Hearing this, my fears quietened a bit, and I got myself together to go grab something to eat. However, when I returned, I caught him talking on the phone to no one else but the woman who had ruined my life for so many months.

As a flood of tears overwhelmed my eyes, I fully realized my husband did not care about me at all because the scene I had just walked into was yet another stab in my back. Yet, I knew that to gain proper closure, I had to know what had been happening, and this time, my best course of action was to contact this woman's girlfriend.

Getting a hold of said girlfriend, I inquired if she knew what exactly her partner and my husband were up to, and she gave me the clarity I had been looking for. She told me she had not seen her partner for a few days, and upon investigating, found out that my husband had been holed up with his former lover in a hotel over the weekend.

The poor girl also told me that she found out my husband had been sleeping with her partner, and it dawned on me when my husband had said he was returning from his mother's, he had been coming back from the hotel he had been staying at where he was cheating on me once again.

I had expected my conversation with the home wrecker's partner to stay private, but I soon found out that my husband knew I had been investigating his actions in secret by the way he unleashed his anger at me. He was so fired up that he started to throw all my belongings in the garage, and I had to call the police to calm him down because I was sure he was going to hurt me.

When the police arrived, they told him he might have to leave for the night to calm down because I was pregnant and had nowhere to go. So, he left and went to his mother's house. In the months that followed, there were many attempts made to patch up our relationship, which in my opinion, was breathing its last. I was right because my husband refused to put in the work, and I went through my pregnancy alone. It was hell; I wish it not on my worst enemy. Thank God, my dad, stepmom, and sister were around to pull me out of the dungeons.

My second baby went through a tough time. In my third trimester, I started to notice itching all over my body. My midwife at the time ordered blood work to figure out what was causing this discomfort, and she told me it was a cholestasis pregnancy where the liver becomes adversely impacted as the baby grows. The condition triggers intense itching on the hands and feet, and other parts of the body. At the time, I was 30 weeks pregnant and about to be induced for labor at 36 weeks.

But I knew something was not right and requested the midwife to put me on a prescription. I was already a high-risk patient due to my rising blood pressure. So, I had to do follow-up visits with my doctor every two weeks, one of which resulted in my obstetrician-gynecologist (OB-GYN) telling me I needed to have an emergency C-section due to preeclampsia.

There was no denying I was stressing out when I was informed of this. Moreover, my husband had recently filed for a divorce, which added to my experience of emotional trauma. Immediately, I had to call my sister, she came with me to the hospital. There, I had my baby Kacie on June 22, 2016.

My miracle child was born premature, but she was strong, and did a good job adapting to the act of breathing at the baby (NICU) Neonatal Intensive Care Unit. I went home for a week, recovered, and went back every day to be by her side to feed her and pray to God to help her develop so she could come home.

AN ENCOUNTER WITH EMBERS – THE DIAGNOSIS THAT SCORCHED MY SOUL

A s the clock went ticking away, turning the days into months and the latter into years, my neck began to feel very uncomfortable.

I did not understand why it hurt unbearably every time I swallowed a morsel of food. It was an unusual feeling, not something I had experienced before. With all the emotional turmoil I have been through, my intuition kicked in soon, and I just knew something was not right at all. But I waited to go get checked out because I just wanted to wait for my baby to be released from the hospital.

It did not take long for Kacie to be home. She was thriving each day! She started eating from a bottle and breathing better, and finally, I decided it was time for me to get my throat and neck problems checked out.

So, I took Kacie home and decided to go visit the emergency room. A computed tomography scan (CT-scan) was the first thing I got done, and while I was waiting for the results, I remember calling my husband at the time and telling him what was happening.

To no one's surprise, my husband was still ice cold towards me of course, I had always expected that the sinking ship was our relationship, and would not rise from the damage so easily. But what I had not accounted for was the fact that even in the clutches of disease, the man I had loved would remain unmoved.

Sitting in that hospital waiting room, I remember talking to a stranger who sat next to me. He had asked me if I was okay since it was obvious that something was wrong with me. Not wanting to give away any hints of weakness, I had told this kind stranger I was okay, but I was not though. All I had wanted, from the core of my heart, was that my husband would stand by my side during this difficult time. But I knew I was fighting a lost battle.

When they say the world comes crashing down, the imagination that accompanies that thought is one where the sky is melting into the Earth. But the number of times my entire cosmos had collapsed, I had realized that the damage is so internal that someone might be struggling to breathe, and nobody would be able to guess.

As I continued to wait for my test results that fateful day, not allowing my expressions to expose my fears, I felt like I was about to go through the havoc that nobody else would be able to save me from. The alarm bells had already started ringing in my mind, even though I did not officially know what was happening to me. At that moment, I felt alone and hurt, and constantly kept questioning what I ever did to deserve this.

The waiting game was getting on my nerves, and after two hours of mentally preparing myself for the results, the nurse practitioner called me into a room and said they saw some masses in my neck. They also told me that they would have to admit me for further examination. Hearing this, at first, I was skeptical. But I knew a thorough medical investigation would be for my own good, especially since I had no idea what was going on.

So, I called my family and told them what the doctors had said they planned to do and informed them I would be back home soon. However, I had not anticipated one night would turn into a whole week!

The day I was admitted, I was first seen by an oncologist, and while I readily allowed the professionals to do their job, I had no clue as to what was going on. My mind was so clouded, worrying about having to raise a new baby without my husband's support, I barely even paid attention to what the oncologist was saying. His words started to ring in my ears though when he said that masses on the neck are a cause for grave concern.

The oncologist proceeded to tell me to find out what was going on in my body, a surgeon was going to come and explain to me what was about to happen. The next morning, I was prepped for another CT-scan which took place quickly and I was sent back to my room.

The following day, my oncologist broke the news to me, a piece of information that felt heavy on my ears because they weren't ready to welcome such insight. I was told that the latest CT-scan had discovered that the lymph nodes in my neck were swollen and that a surgical procedure known as a neck dissection was required to gain further clarity.

The doctors said they don't usually perform a neck dissection on every patient. However, in my case, they had considered the prospect carefully and decided that the procedure was necessary to determine if there were cancer cells in my lymph nodes.

I was informed about the risks, while simultaneously being told that lymph cells from my neck would be extracted and sent to the lab for further testing.

As the doctors hovered around me, I felt like things were moving so fast that I did not even have time to properly internalize everything. In what seemed like no time at all, I was prepared for surgery.

Three days after the surgery, I was seen by both my surgeon and my oncologist, who had come to check on me to see how I was feeling. How would someone who just wanted some respite in life feel when they were being met with constant tribulations? Frustrated is one answer that comes to mind, but I was feeling much too helpless and lonely at this point.

When the fourth post-surgery day arrived, I was told I had to get a bone marrow aspiration. This meant I needed local anesthesia to get the procedure done. The fourth day quickly turned into the fifth and I was prepped for yet another procedure that would see pins and needles going into my body.

The bone marrow aspiration took about an hour. I was told to lie on my side, with my knees tucked up into my chest, the doctor numbed the area to reduce pain. Following this, a lumbar puncture was performed by putting a needle into my spine and sucking into a syringe, a fluid known as cerebrospinal fluid. I was alert about what was happening, but I had to lay still and not move, so I did the best I could.

As I was going through the procedure, I remember how gently one of my nurses held my hands. I also remember feeling a sharp pain and tears flowing down my face, but I knew I had to brave the storm.

Once the surgery was over, I stayed in recovery for an hour, as my biopsy results were sent to the labs where healthcare folks would check if my marrow were working the way it is supposed to.

It was one rough week. I was all alone, and the only people who came to see me were my cousins and my sister. Now, I oftentimes look back and just think of the goodness of God who gave me the strength and courage I needed to get through one of the hardest times in my life.

After the whirlwind of surgeries and doctors' visits, it was finally time to go home. As I was being released from the hospital, I was going to call a cab, but to my surprise, my husband called me and told me that he would pick me up and take me home.

It was a sad ride home, mixed emotions, it was a cold ride home, I felt like I didn't know him anymore. Upon entering my husband's vehicle, I immediately smelled cigarette smoke, and I remember asking him what the smell was since I had not remembered him as a smoker. Nonchalant, he had responded by saying that it was not him who smoked in the car but his girlfriend.

I was shocked, of course, thinking that after everything that had happened, my husband just could not let go of another woman. Gripped by my thoughts, I remember having told him this was the life he had chosen for himself and succumbing to silence after uttering these words.

I had started to wonder whatever happened to the vows that we had made for better or for worse, and as I thanked my husband for the ride, I started mentally preparing myself for the weeks ahead.

I had to do a follow-up visit with my oncologist. When the day of the visit came, my stepmother said that she wanted to accompany me to the appointment as moral support. I met with the doctor, and everything he explained to me was a blur. Yet, I could make out the fact I had been diagnosed with Hodgkin's Lymphoma stage 2.

Hodgkin's lymphoma is a type of lymphoma in which cancer originates from a specific type of white blood cells called lymphocytes. Lymphocytes are one of several different types of white blood cells. Each type of white blood cell has a specific function, and they all work together to fight illness and disease. As cancer progresses, it limits the body's ability to fight infection. White blood cells are an important part of your immune system. They help your body fight antigens, which are bacteria, viruses, and other toxins that make you sick. My doctor advised that I have a weakened immune system, which means there are not enough white blood cells in my bloodstream.

However, the good news is that Hodgkin's disease is considered one of the most treatable forms of cancer if found early. Mine had been discovered at the second stage, which meant it was treatable, but who wants to hear the word 'cancer'?

I could never have imagined being diagnosed with this disease, especially not while I was going through a divorce. My husband went and filed paperwork to walk away from his marriage. I just remember wondering how much more I could take in terms of sorrow and turmoil, and my shock was so apparent on my face that I am sure I must have laughed out loud in disbelief.

Life is what it is though, and I had to deal with the fact I had cancer now. My family perhaps had even more of a hard time coming to terms with the diagnosis. I remember when I told my sister, she exclaimed, "The devil is a liar." My father, his grief could not be matched.

WALKING ON JAGGED COBBLESTONES

If I had expected my husband at the time to have any semblance of a soft heart, I was proved wrong again and again. One would think that when someone has just been diagnosed with cancer, their partner would feel an ounce of compassion for them. Yet, in my partner's case, this did not apply.

Given how unsupportive my husband was after the diagnosis, I still had to face my battles, the most jarring of which was the fight to stay in my home with my two children. This was a fight I knew I had to win, because the alternative was for my children to become homeless. I was fed up with living here, there, and everywhere and just wanted to be able to settle down, but that seemed like an impossible goal to achieve.

Every day after the diagnosis, I would get harassed to move out and find somewhere else to call home. I truly wanted to escape from Florida at that point, because I felt like I could not take any more trauma. My sense of desperation forced me to call and reach out to every single person I could think of. At this point, pride was out the door.

I tried friends who my mother had helped when they needed a place to live, the family who I thought would take me, and generally anyone I could recall who had ever sought support from us. No one was willing to take us in, though, and I would cry myself to sleep many nights.

At this point in my life, I was just astonished by how cruel and heartless people could be. Yet, I was not ready to believe that humans, the beautiful creations of God were made of ice-cold souls. So, I attributed the actions of those who hurt me to the work of the devil and his counterparts.

When I reflected on my husband's actions and those of his new girlfriend, it was painful to see how two people fought so hard to be together, especially a woman fighting another woman for a man that is still married. But they didn't care at all. It was evident they just wanted to be together and had no remorse or compassion for me.

At one point, things got so hard that my parents wanted to leave after all that was going on around us. At first, I was heartbroken, wondering why my own parents would give up on me when I needed their strength and prayers. But God was on my side, and He led my parents to stay with me.

Every day seemed like yet another chore. The mornings, evenings, and nights were filled with my husband's voice as it would tell me to move into another room so he could move in. In his words, summer was almost over, and school was about to start. So, everyone needed to be comfortable. He had his children, and his lover was pregnant at the time.

Due to this, he had to move her out of his parent's house and make her comfortable. The idea was that since we were getting a divorce, I would have to be the one who would be kicked out of the house as soon as the divorce was final so that my husband could stay there with his new girlfriend.

Initially, I had thought that had lost his mind when he gave me this ultimatum, but I soon realized he meant every word. Despite this, I did not take him seriously until I was at home and saw him coming into the house with his girlfriend. I remember asking her why she would allow my husband to have her leave the place she was staying at so easily. In response, she told me she had refused the prospect; however, since it was the only way my husband could bring this woman into my house and push me out, he had started using intimidation to force the former to give in.

In the days that followed, they officially moved in. To this day, I still believe this was the craziest thing a wife could experience in her own home. Every night, my husband slept with his new girlfriend in our marital room, the one we had once shared as a couple. Neither he nor his girlfriend cared about the complete collapse of morality they were setting an example for, but this new arrangement didn't last too long.

One day, I recall that some mail had come to the house. I had opened the door to collect it, but before I could even understand what was happening, the new girlfriend came running down the stairs and grabbed it from me, without even saying thank you! That is when I completely lost it.

I think this moment was a reality check for me because I was supposed to portray this pure persona, which implied because I was a Christian, I should not act out or fight, or I should allow the Lord to fight my battles. But by this time, I had enough.

Like a scene in a movie, I remember myself marching up the stairs and banging on the door. In an angry tirade, I gave her a piece of my mind, demanding how she had dared to let a man move her into his wife's house. At this moment, she had locked herself into our room, and my stepmother begged me to stop arguing and held me back because I was ready to fight. I had enough, and I knew this home-wrecking woman had to leave.

I was not afraid and intimidated any more. At that point, I think I found my strength because I did not know which way to turn. My mind kept swirling with thoughts about how this woman could come into my house and how I could just sit and take it.

So, I told her the facts exactly as they were. I told her I was so hurt this was happening to me. I asked her how she could be so heartless. Finally, I said if she wanted my husband that was fine, and she could have him, but she had to go and live her own life instead of allowing him to move her into his wife's home.

I also dealt a big blow to the girlfriend by saying she was a woman with children, and I couldn't believe she was letting a man control her in this manner as it would set a horrible example for her kids. In hindsight, I realize I would never dish such a lashing out to my worst enemy, but my nerves had reached their saturation point, and the pent-up anger had needed some release.

A few days later, the woman I had bludgeoned with my words left and never came back. My husband was very upset with me about it. He also felt betrayed by his girlfriend because, he had done everything to prove his love, and she had still left him like a fool.

I know my husband was fuming, afraid of his tantrums, I had even called the police for help, but they had told me they couldn't do anything unless a crime scene was part of the story. I was truly sad, but now my only option left was a restraining order.

Knowing the next step, I had to take, I went to the court and filed two separate restraining orders, one for my husband, and one for his girlfriend so that both would stay away from me. To my surprise, I discovered the woman had beaten me to it. Because she was already upset, she had lied and filed for a restraining order against me!

As the story goes, while I was filing a restraining order against the woman, I was approached by a sheriff who served me papers with the order she had filed. According to her terms, she had stated that because she wasn't in the home where I lived anymore, she didn't want me around her children.

This was almost laughable because I had been raising the children she had with my husband for so long. I had been the one taking them to school, doing my part as a mother and a wife.

The conditions were beyond me, and it was the highest level of evil I could ever imagine. All I had wanted was peace and for my husband and his girlfriend to leave me alone. Yet, she had thought that lying and making up stories to keep me away from her children since I was still married was worth it. God was on my side though as became clear in the court proceedings that followed.

Once the papers went through, at the scheduled hearing date, I ended up going to court. There, the girlfriend told her side of the story, and I told mine. I explained to the judge what had been happening.

I described how my husband and I were going through a divorce and how this woman wanted me out of the house so that she could move in. Then, I stated that she had moved in, and we had gotten into a fight because I was not leaving my own home. The judge saw the truth in my statements, he then went out to say we both seem like nice women, but he strictly warned us to leave each other alone and threw the case out.

I breathed a sigh of relief, but the storm had not yet passed.

One day, I left the house to go visit one of my cousins. In my absence, my husband went into the room I was staying in and searched it through and through. As he snooped around, he found papers to the petitions I had filed as well as the restraining order. The papers had not officially been served to him yet, so he was taken aback, and his fury reared its head again.

When I got back to the house, my husband confronted me about the papers he had found, and like a madman, saying how could I do such a thing to him, when he was thinking about making things work between us. I was taken back by that statement because of all that has happened, he started to make me feel so bad, but he knew why I had to do it and why it was done. I was so confused and just broken to pieces; I couldn't believe all of this was happening to my life.

IRRECONCILABLE DIFFERENCES

Divorce was approaching. It was hurtling towards me like a bullet train, and I felt like I was just standing at the station with all my baggage, unsure of where I would go once I boarded the vehicle.

Communication between my husband and I was nearly non-existent at this point. I can recall as clear as day, the night before our hearing date. I remember I was crying and begging him not to leave me. Even though so much time has passed, I still mourn the fact that we were not able to make things work.

At the time, I felt so weak and helpless that I decided I needed my husband more than anything else.

We had been through so much together, had shared some great memories, and we finally were getting ahead in life. I mean, when we met, we had nothing to our name and now we had accomplished so much together. Internalizing all this made me realize that the devil was just simply trying to rip our marriage apart.

Yet, I knew that questioning fate wouldn't change it. My husband was very vocal about the fact that he said he was done.

According to him, we had grown apart, and he wanted someone who was going to keep it real with him. He said he wanted someone who was from the streets. It haunts me he made such a monumental decision without really thinking about how I would raise two little girls on my own.

But I knew that I had to stay strong, get myself together, and move on. After all, I had cancer to combat and defeat as well. So, the night before our hearing, I cried myself to sleep.

The next day, I woke up, got dressed, and started to make my way to the court that would tell us how the divorce proceedings would be finalized.

As if on cue, my husband's new girlfriend showed up as I was approaching the gate of our house. She was pulling up to take her kids to school, and as her eyes landed on me, she showed me the nasty middle finger.

At that moment, I remember thinking to myself that this woman surely got what she wanted. In hindsight, whenever I reflect upon the scene, I remind myself to be grateful I had never taken what I wanted by stealing things that belonged to other people. It would never have sat well in my conscience. The guilt would have laid ruin to the crevices of my mind until it began to rot.

Fast forward to the courthouse where my husband and I met in the presence of our mediator. As the meeting progressed, we went over all the relevant legal details that would finalize the divorce. At one point, the mediator asked my husband if he was sure he didn't want to reconcile. With a tone that can best be defined as frosty, my husband had responded, saying indeed, he was sure.

In my heart, I was still willing to work with my husband, especially about child support and parental visitation. Even in those dark days, I didn't hate the man. He was still the same man who had fallen in love with me, and I found myself still reciprocating love despite the distance between us.

Our mediator was shocked I was willing to be so kind and cooperate with my husband despite everything that happened in our relationship. She even articulated her surprise as she turned to me and said it was mighty nice of me to want to work with my husband after all we both have been through.

As for me, I knew that my sense of compassion was driven by the fact I wasn't bitter but I was hurting. In no way, shape, or form was I out to get the man who had fathered my children.

After the mediation, my husband wanted to finalize the divorce immediately. He asked for the judge to sign off on the papers the very same day, and when that was achieved, we went our separate ways within the next few hours.

As soon as we got the divorce, my ex-husband moved out and started working with his girlfriend to find a place to live. I discovered that they did manage to put together a place after all, because one day, there was a knock on my door that revealed a police escort who was accompanying my former partner, his girlfriend, and another friend of theirs to my house.

The policeman had been part of the story at this point due to the restraining order I had filed against my ex-husband. As I opened the door, I realized the group had come over to get all my ex's furniture and personal belongings from my house so that they could be shifted to their new abode.

Reality hit me hard that day. It finally sank in that the man who was rushing around and bagging his belongings was now my ex-husband. He couldn't have been crueler though.

As I sat watching with my mouth open, he proceeded to move everything out of the house. There wasn't even a sofa left for my daughters and me to sit on. The TV my girls loved to watch was also snatched away from us. To put the icing on the cake, when my ex and his girlfriend were done hoarding the stuff, they got their kids together and laughed in my face before they stepped out the door.

I know that they were seeking a reaction, anything to see if I had been broken and beaten by my ex yet. But I was smart. I didn't make any fuss about the whole situation. Besides, I reminded myself that all the things my ex had taken were owned by him anyway. He had bought them with the money he earned, and if I tried to claim them, I would just be perceived as greedy.

Plus, I knew that I had no reason to keep his belongings, for we were no longer together, and any time we did cross paths, it would just be for co-parenting purposes.

It didn't take long for the divorce to shuffle to the back of my mind. I had other, more important things to worry about. My health was a priority now, and I had to make sure cancer exited my body so I could be there to watch my girls grow up.

As worries plagued my soul, God showed me once again that He is the Universal Healer. He opened a family friend's heart to me, which made my life a little easier.

The friend in question was moving at the time. Due to this, she had a spare couch and a dining set she was looking to give away. She offered the items to me and my girls, and I was so grateful we accepted the favor with enthusiasm. I knew then that the Divine Father was still and would always be in control.

THE ART OF INDEPENDENCE

The lymph node on the left side of my neck was growing bigger as time progressed. My skin had also started to itch really bad, and to hide the hint of cancer on my skin, I had started wearing only turtlenecks and long sleeves.

As the days passed by, my skin began to change color too. I was darker than I normally would look. I was losing weight. I was skinny. Yet, I didn't look sick, so no one could tell something was wrong with me until I told them.

In the throes of sickness, I fully recognized I was alone, with two children to look after, I had to take matters into my hands and secure our financial independence. If I didn't do this, we wouldn't be able to survive.

Those years are etched in my mind like a poignant memory.

During the difficult days, to make some money, I would go out and do food delivery, Postmates, and Uber. I had a truck I had financed, and I had to keep up with the payments. I got that truck while I was still married, when I found out I was expecting a child, my ex-husband and I decided we needed a bigger vehicle for the family.

Money had trickled in before too. But everything I experienced had taught me that while a dollar was a tangible object, it was fleeting. Wealth, I noticed, could come and go in the blink of an eye and we just had to accept this reality.

For instance, I know how excited I was when I once got a new job at the doctor's office. This was back when I was pregnant as well. With this new work assignment, I assumed my financial woes would cease, but I was wrong because the job didn't last long. After all, I ended up being late to work one day.

At the time, I was on a 90-day probation. One of those days, I had to take my ex's daughter to school for registration. Due to this, I couldn't make it to the office on time, a few minutes after I got in, I was advised I should leave and go home.

I was gutted, of course. I had never wanted to leave the job. But this instance was a huge wake-up call for me, and I understood I needed to strive harder to be more independent and financially stable.

CLAIMING MY PLACE AND POWER-ONE STEP AT A TIME

Increased awareness and pursuit of independence steered me towards education as well. Following the divorce, I quickly decided I might as well enroll in a high school program, Penn Foster. I got my high school diploma and that made me feel so good, I felt so free, it was as if a burden was lifted off my shoulders and with my diploma at hand, I was able to use it and enroll in college and earned a degree that would qualify me to work as a medical field associate.

My dreams of investing in academic endeavors came to fruition in form of a Health Science degree at the Ultimate Medical Academy. Thankfully, the program was offered online, so it was easy for me to participate since I could study and attend to my children at the same time.

Following my divorce, I also decided not to renew the lease in the old apartment. It was time to move on, I remember seeing a quote that empowered me to keep pushing and it says, "Don't be afraid to start over, you just might like your new life better," and so my sister, being the true gem she is, found a great realtor to help me with the process. I believe it was divine because soon enough I started checking out some new places where my daughters and I could start afresh.

Humans can plan, but ultimately God is the greatest planner. All this time, He already knew where I would be living with my children after the divorce devastation. By this time, I had become a United States Citizen. In a fascinating turn of events, the area I went to get my citizenship from was right across the building where I received my citizenship interview. This building housed an apartment that would eventually end up in my possession.

When I first laid eyes on that apartment, I was moved because I had never expected I would approve of living in such a place. But this unit had been vacant for a while, and when the realtor made an offer, I could not refuse, I accepted this wonderful new house with joy. I barely was making ends meet, all I had was faith and I trust God in His infinite power to work it out for us and He came through for me and the girls, all I could remember in my messed-up self was, thank You, God.

In the meantime, I cleaned the old apartment, laundered the musty carpets, and performed general handyman repairs in the house I was leaving behind. So, when it was time for inspection, I was sure I had done a commendable job in fixing the place up for a new family to inhabit it. My intuition was correct, and I passed the inspection with flying colors. I was looking forward to getting all my deposits back on the apartment to buy new pieces of furniture and start afresh.

It took about a month or two before I heard anything about my deposit. At the time, I was staying with a family member who was kind enough to allow me to live with her until the new apartment was ready for the girls and me.

As I waited for the matter to proceed, certain alarm bells started ringing in my mind, and I began to feel like perhaps I might not be able to transition out of the old house as smoothly as I had expected.

Lo and behold, my gut feeling had hit the nail on the head because I ended up doing some online research on the management company that owned the townhouse I used to live in, I discovered that it was a fraud.

During my research, I stumbled upon some really bad reviews about the company in question. The people it had ripped off stated that the entity stole deposits and ran away with the money. Reeling with this information, I wrote a furious email to the company demanding that they return my money. No response came.

Ultimately, I had to call the management and they told me, unfortunately, I had not passed the inspection after all. Due to this, I would only be receiving one hundred dollars from the three thousand six hundred dollars I had deposited because the management claimed they had to make deductions for all the cleaning they had to do themselves, but I passed the inspection. How is this possible? I was astonished at how unprofessional they handled the process and the lies and wickedness behind everything their company does.

Indeed, it was frustrating to discover that so much of my hard-earned money had gone down the drain, but I held onto the hope that life would get better as we moved into our new apartment.

The big day finally came when my girls and I shifted to our new home. The home was part of a nice condo community near a lake. It was built in a very pleasant, open style, which allowed for thorough ventilation.

The move was easy for us because we didn't have too many belongings. All we had were our clothes, a few pieces of furniture, a table, a couch, a mattress, a baby bassinet, and a toddler bed. Even with our small luggage, I had kept most of the items in storage and had to go back and forth to fish them all out all by myself, and I also had a family friend help with the couch.

The night we moved, I remember I had been so involved in emptying the storage, I didn't have anything to serve myself and my girls for dinner. But the relative I had been staying with was kind enough to offer we eat something before we go, and I was so thankful God was still supporting me every step of the way.

God's uncommon favors continued to shine brightly upon me. The first day I sat on my couch in our new home, I looked at my phone and saw an email that came bearing great news.

At the time, I had a prepaid card I had used at my old job for direct deposit. The email I stumbled across informed me my bank account had been credited with a deposit of four thousand five hundred dollars ($4500). To say that I was in utter disbelief would be an understatement.

In a daze, I remember logging into my account to confirm what this deposit was for; doing so made me realize a company I had been working for had sent the money because it owed me some financial returns.

Losing money to a fraudulent home management company and then receiving it from an organization was a miracle; it is something I am still grateful for to this day.

Suddenly, I wasn't traumatized by a crippling fear of scarcity. I realized at that moment I could spend a little cash to make our new home comfortable for myself and my girls.

Excitedly, I started visiting department stores to look for suitable furniture and was able to get a family discount from Walmart and through this discount, I purchased a TV which I complemented with a TV stand from IKEA.

Moreover, during my shopping spree, I came across a young lady who was selling a bed frame, according to her, the frame was in tip-top condition because it had never been used, upon seeing the golden opportunity to fix up my bed, I bought this frame too. In the days that followed, my sister made several visits to help me polish the house and transform it into my dream home.

HICCUPS ALONG THE WAY

The cancer was getting worse, and I still didn't have the financial clearance to start my treatment.

As my skin itched until I wanted to scratch it into oblivion, I realized with more clarity how much power money holds in this world. Constantly in and out of hospitals, I remember vividly how many of these auspicious institutions readily kicked me out without helping me simply because I couldn't afford the medical bills.

Every time I was turned away by yet another doctor, I would go back home, fall apart in my living room and cry till the tears ran out.

It felt like my world would end at any given second because the pain and discomfort became so unbearable. As the itching intensified, I recall that I would scratch my limbs to the point where they would bleed.

Nevertheless, I knew I couldn't give up because the cancer was a battle I couldn't afford to lose. I had two children to raise, after all.

With a limited income, it wasn't easy to raise my girls at the time. Usually, I had to wait until my girls visited their father because that is when I would get time to go out and make some money. During those years, I was still doing Postmates and Uber and had to get by on whatever I managed to earn after putting in long days of work.

My body continued to fail me. I remember how I would take at least three showers a day to ease the symptoms. At nights, I would cough so bad that I felt like I was going to die. But it was in those moments I truly reconnected with God, for I felt the way His healing Hand held me steadily through the turmoil.

One night during my worship, the presence of the Heavenly Father filled the room. He spoke into my heart as I worshipped along watching Hill Song Channel with the Hillsong team.

That day, I immediately sensed the anointing of God, giving me peace and hope. The songs, "What a Beautiful Name," and "Let There Be Light," especially ministered to me. Right there in my living room, I experienced something so supernatural that my belief was reinforced that God is real and I'm a living testimony of His grace and healing power.

Armed with my renewed faith in God's support, I know I needed to strive once again to find a doctor who would help me. So, I drove myself to a local hospital and got checked out. I was admitted and seen by an oncologist, but unfortunately, this place also sent me packing because I still didn't have my insurance.

However, this hospital wasn't as ruthless as the others had been, and it sent me to an institution that could help me out.

RE-EMERGENCE: LIKE A PHOENIX, RISE, AND TAKE FLIGHT

s I followed the hospital's directions, I ended up being referred to an oncologist who was perfectly equipped to take care of me. God also aligned my affairs in a manner where I got approved for insurance to start my treatment, the first time I went to see this Godsent doctor, I felt a great sense of peace over me, and knew that I was going to be in good hands; immediately, the whole team got me registered and prepared to get a chemo port installed in my chest following chemo treatments.

At this point, I was sure it was meant to be, that things were bound to fall into place. I knew that the answer to my loved ones' prayers was fast approaching, and everyone dear to me would get to see me heal.

Throughout my journey, I have had people who were holding the intention for me to experience the vigor of life once again.

These folks had been praying for me and helping me get through this rough time, even when they had been total strangers or friends who lived afar. The people God sent to elevate me, my church family, standing in agreement for healing in my body, cheering me on and believing God for my body's complete healing.

I was ready to start a brand-new chapter, one that did not carry the shame I felt due to my darkening skin complexion and blackened nails. By this time, I had also lost a lot of weight. My hair was also falling out, and I just did not feel beautiful at all.

Over time, you accept the fact cancer will change your body, but there aren't people who talk about how they feel about their body changes. If you ask me, it hurts really bad when you don't recognize the person you see in the mirror now.

When sickness is messing with your peace of mind, and the reflection you see in the mirror every day, it is easy to feel hopeless; yet God gave me the strength to encourage myself every day. Soon, I wasn't bothered about the way I looked anymore because the only acceptance I was looking for is from my Creator, and He loves everyone regardless of their skin, hair, and nails.

My worries were further alleviated by the kindness of my oncologist. I remember during my initial visit to see him, he had seen my swollen lymph node and told me not to worry because, in a month, the node would be gone, and the itching would be eradicated.

This wonderful doctor is named Atif Hussein, and his wonderful PA Jorge Adames one of the best Oncologists at Memorial Regional Hospital in Hollywood, Florida. To this day, I am so thankful to him and his whole staff for taking such good care of me. It's amazing how some people can come into your life for a little while and make the biggest changes to it. Yet we often don't value their efforts and consider what they do as part of their jobs.

For my treatment, I had to do blood work and get my port flushed, which was followed by regular doses of chemo meds. I had to get Benadryl for the side effects because, after a treatment session, I would be sick for a whole week. But I didn't let these adverse effects interfere with my daily life. I still cooked and cleaned and did everything a mother is supposed to do while simultaneously finishing my assignments for school.

To say that managing all my responsibilities at that point in my life was hard work would be an understatement, but what got me through was God and God alone. His light shone through me and for me, lighting up the way as treatment progressed, inspiring not just me, but also everyone around me.

I remember going into chemo one day and one of the nurses asked me how I was doing. In response, I told her I was doing great with a smile on my face. She had smiled back and said it was good to hear I was recuperating.

Moving on, she had asked me if I got nauseous or sick, to which I had responded by saying "not anymore."

It's these little acts of kindness that can make anyone's day, and showing compassion to others regardless of their condition can go a long way in elevating your mood.

As soon as I told her this, I could tell that she was surprised, and even more so when I told her I had to pick myself up right after treatment because I had to go back home, take care of my kids, cook dinner, focus on school, and prioritize earning an income for my family. As the nurse heard me out, she had this stunned expression on her face, and when I was done talking, she exclaimed an energetic "Wow!"

The nurse then asked me if I was a Believer, without hesitation, I told her I was. I also told her my faith in Jesus was the #1 reason why I could go on despite excruciating pain and insurmountable challenges.

The same faith, I told her, was what kept me motivated and standing firm on the Word of God. The sweet nurse told me that hearing my story gave her goosebumps. She also proceeded to say the very reason why she comes to work every day was to minister to someone. To her, the job wasn't about the money or the degree.

My God! I realized internally; this nurse was such a humble sweet soul. We connected on a spiritual level. That's when I knew God had me at the right place at the right time to connect with people who would help me get through this season.

This nurse is only one member of that tribe of amazing individuals who got me through the storm. My sister is another such person. She helped me with my children when I would be gone for treatment. Close to her nieces, she would always be there to hang out with them. She would also give me some cheerful company when my girls stayed with their dad. We would have slumber parties and watch movies together, making sure we had something fun and interesting to do in those difficult times.

My sister brought me so much joy that it did take my mind off of everything. The chemo was also starting to show results at this point. I was getting better and better and didn't even have to stop my college courses. I just kept going because I was determined to finish up and graduate.

As of March 20, 2018, I'm cancer-free! The day is engraved in my memory with the purest gold and the most exhilarating sense of happiness I have ever felt. Marked with a certificate in Chemotherapy completion from Memorial Regional Cancer Center, the experience of defeating a deadly illness will be one I will always remember for its devastating yet humbling side effects.

Cancer will always remain a foe, but I will also recall it with a perspective that is defined by strength, wisdom, and the courage to face every obstacle life throws at me.

The certificate in question is a reminder of the grit I had to inculcate in myself to combat the illness. As a token that their mother survived immense hardships, I passed on the document to my girls as a gift. Being too young, they didn't understand what this piece of paper meant, but I am sure its value will become evident as they grow up.

A month after I was deemed cancer-free, I graduated from college on April 21, 2018. As I walk down memory lane recalling my graduation, I remember gracing the stage and receiving my Associate's degree in front of my biggest supporters: my dad, stepmom, my two girls, and my sister, all of whom had made so many sacrifices for me, and their presence at the occasion meant the world to me.

Currently, the cancer is in remission. My health is back, the hair on my head has started to grow back, my nails cleared up, and my skin complexion has gone back to being normal, I have gained back weight. The hardest part of the treatment I had to undergo was completed through radiation therapy. This was targeted at shrinking the remaining tumors in my chest. This therapy took a month to complete, and I had to have sessions five days a week.

The initial visits I made to the doctor for radiation therapy were focused on gathering all the information about my medical demographics and to meet with the radiation oncologist, who then explained the procedures.

Because I had to get radiation in my chest, I had to get a custom-made thermoplastic mask to fit my face to wear during simulation and treatment sessions. The procedure was very uncomfortable.

During my sessions, I would lie on my back, and my radiation mask would gently hold my head in place, helping me to remain in the correct position to ensure the laser beam could isolate the area of my skin it was working on. Nearly every day, for about 30 minutes, I would put myself through this unpleasant experience. Needless to say, I was quite miserable. But I went through the process and completed my one month of treatment because, at the end of it, a normal life stood waving at me in excitement and anticipation.

When I was declared free from cancer, my creative juices started to flow, and I started a T-shirt brand called Kingdom Culture Couture. Inspired by God's Grace, which uplifted me as I fought a deadly disease, I wanted to encourage others to be similarly inspired. With this objective in mind, I began to design apparels, which reflected a Believer's love for Jesus. My business soon took off and started crushing new milestones.

As I drove past all the hardships, I always kept an eye on the rear-view mirror, remembering each and every day of my journey and how I became this person. This is where I wanted to be and with everything that happened in my life, I never imagined I would be here. This is the power of faith, and considering where it got me, I don't think I could have imagined a better way.

However, I know better than most what it feels like to live blindly, so my journey will continue to the last day of my life. Until that moment comes, there are many things I have yet to experience, but I know this time, I have God by my side, so whatever problems and hardships that await me, they better be ready for me and my Lord.

A LIFE TODAY

At present, I am enrolled in South Florida Bible College for my Bachelor's in ministry and leadership. I first began to invest my time and effort in this endeavor because I discovered I have a passion for Christian motivational speaking and vocalizing the powerful Word of God.

To pursue a Bachelor's degree under consideration, I didn't wish to enroll in college. However, when God told me to go back to school, I said to myself even though I had felt like I was done with school after acquiring an Associate's degree; If the Heavenly Father wanted me to pursue more learning, then I was ready to do so.

As I delve deeper into inquiring about the word of God, I am sure that opting for this course of study has been the best decision I have ever made. Perhaps there is no better way to describe the sense of accomplishment I feel than saying that I am engulfed by a deep peace, knowing I am on the right path; one that is devoid of rocky pebbles and lined with the most beautiful flowers. God is holding my hand and taking care of my journey onwards...

In the Holy Book, God says: "And after you have suffered a little while, the God of all grace, who has called you to his eternal glory in Christ, will himself restore, confirm, strengthen, and establish you." 1 Peter 5:10.

The statement captures God's promise. It outlines what is coming for those who put their faith in His power to pull you out of the darkest dungeons and surround you with the brightest light.

I am very grateful as I celebrate life, for I know it is a blessing I must not take for granted. Fighting not just a disease, but also socio-economic and relationship-related hardships, I also believe I have developed a great deal of empathy for others who may be experiencing one or all the same things I had to pull through.

I'd like to think I have become a very compassionate person, mainly because I can relate to anyone going through the same things I went through or any other hardship. It is difficult for people to talk about the battles they're fighting in their daily lives, even with close friends, partners, or family. Whether it's shame or sorrow, people end up keeping all their troubles to themselves.

Understanding this, I would also like to celebrate the journeys of my fellow travelers and offer them my support to whatever extent possible. I believe once we program our minds to face our adversities and get through the hurdles and strife of life, we emerge not only victorious, but decked out in pure gold.

Cancer is only going to be a chapter in your life, not the whole story. So, in between the bad and worse times, look deep into yourself and find the light because it may be your only chance to survive. Having the right people in your life when you need them will help, but at the end of it all, you'll be the one fighting alongside God.

I survived because the fire inside burned brighter than the fire around. Speaking through the lessons I have learned based on my reality, I can say for certain, once the storm is over, you won't remember how you made it through, or how you managed to survive. You won't even be sure whether the storm is over, but one thing is certain; when you come out of the storm, you won't be the same person who walked in. That's what this storm's all about!

And I'm confident there are thousands of people who have experienced something similar and or are currently fighting their own battles. Coming back from war changes the toughest of soldiers and at the same time, a mere heartbreak could make people lose themselves completely. Whatever the case is, there are people out there that are constantly facing their demons and finding themselves within.

Perhaps people need to understand what it means to find satisfaction consistently so they can focus on surviving sailing through the deepest oceans instead of looking for land. Maybe we're so focused on instant gratification we hurt ourselves thinking about our journey. We want everything right away; whether it's food, clothes, happiness, and pleasure, and when we fail to get it, we lose ourselves.

I can't remember the countless times I thought about a life in which I didn't get abused, or where my parents never got separated. If we remain fixated on wishful thinking, we neglect our present and add to our grief. Remember every part of your journey and face every obstacle as they come. By focusing on the finish line, we forget where we are and start thinking about winning and losing, and not the race. And this is where we begin to doubt ourselves.

Whenever you find yourself doubting how far you can go, just remember how far you have come. Remember everything you have faced, all the battles you have won, and all the fears you have overcome. Tell yourself: I'm a warrior, I'm stronger than I've ever been. Cancer may have started the fight, but I am the one who finishes it, and I am the one who comes out stronger!

My experience has molded me and shaped me into the Woman God destined me to be. I now have a passion for helping others. As a cancer survivor, I now see what my calling is and where my motivations will take me.

I would never have chosen cancer. However, cancer has become the crucible for growth in my relationship with God and learning, God is good all the time! I can now say (and mean it!),

"Thank you, God for what having cancer has taught me, about who You are, and that Your grace is more than sufficient."

Perhaps I cannot even fully express the sentiments cancer has led me to feel, but once again, the Word of God suffices to help me articulate my feelings. Ecclesiastes 5:20 sums up both the emotional and spiritual side effects of chemo on my life: "For he will not much remember the bad days of his life because God keeps him occupied with joy in his heart."

Throughout my journey, I experienced so much joy and uncommon favor, I do not doubt in my heart, God is truly amazing. After all, despite the brazen and earth-shattering misadventures, here I am today, in good health and good spirits, typing away this story to share with you, King Jesus and His marvelous ways!

As you move forward with life and the burdens it carries, remember this: If there are giants in your promised land, and God says you can have what you set your heart on, expect EVERY giant to fall! If you operate with this belief, you will see that the testing of your faith produces endurance.

In many ways, the Lord chooses who He loves most and puts them through hardships to help them find Him and become closer. Throughout the hardships, the pain, and the struggles, it is He who carves our path and guides us on it without us even knowing it. We think to ourselves we're in control of our situation, but nothing happens without His will. I had to get cancer to become the person I am today and find my Creator.

To all those reading this right now, have a conversation with your Creator. Allow your inner dialogue to flow without boundaries and say: God, I refuse to be defeated and intimidated by the opposition that has come to challenge me. You said in Your Word that all things are possible with You. Today, I believe You have equipped me to slay every giant in my life and possess the promises You have spoken over me. So, I resist fear and walk by faith in my destiny.

The path from a damaged childhood to a healed adult is filled with potholes, landmines, and obstacles, and walking on them is not for the faint-hearted. While it sometimes seems avoiding our pain of the past is the path of least resistance, it could lead to prolonged suffering that comes from the resistance to life itself.

From the separation of my parents to everything I have suffered till now, one would think my life would turn out hopeless, and I would die a painful and miserable death with no friends, family, or loved ones. If I had denied my pain through whatever means I chose to employ, only God knows what grievances I could have suffered from.

So, submit your will to the Creator and let Him guide you on the path He already chose for you. In the end, all that will matter is your connection with Him because we came into this world alone, and we will leave this world alone, so remember Him in everything you do, and everywhere you go, because He remembers you.